I0468971

Swear Word Coloring Book

SWEARING FAIRIES

SWEAR WORD COLORING BOOK

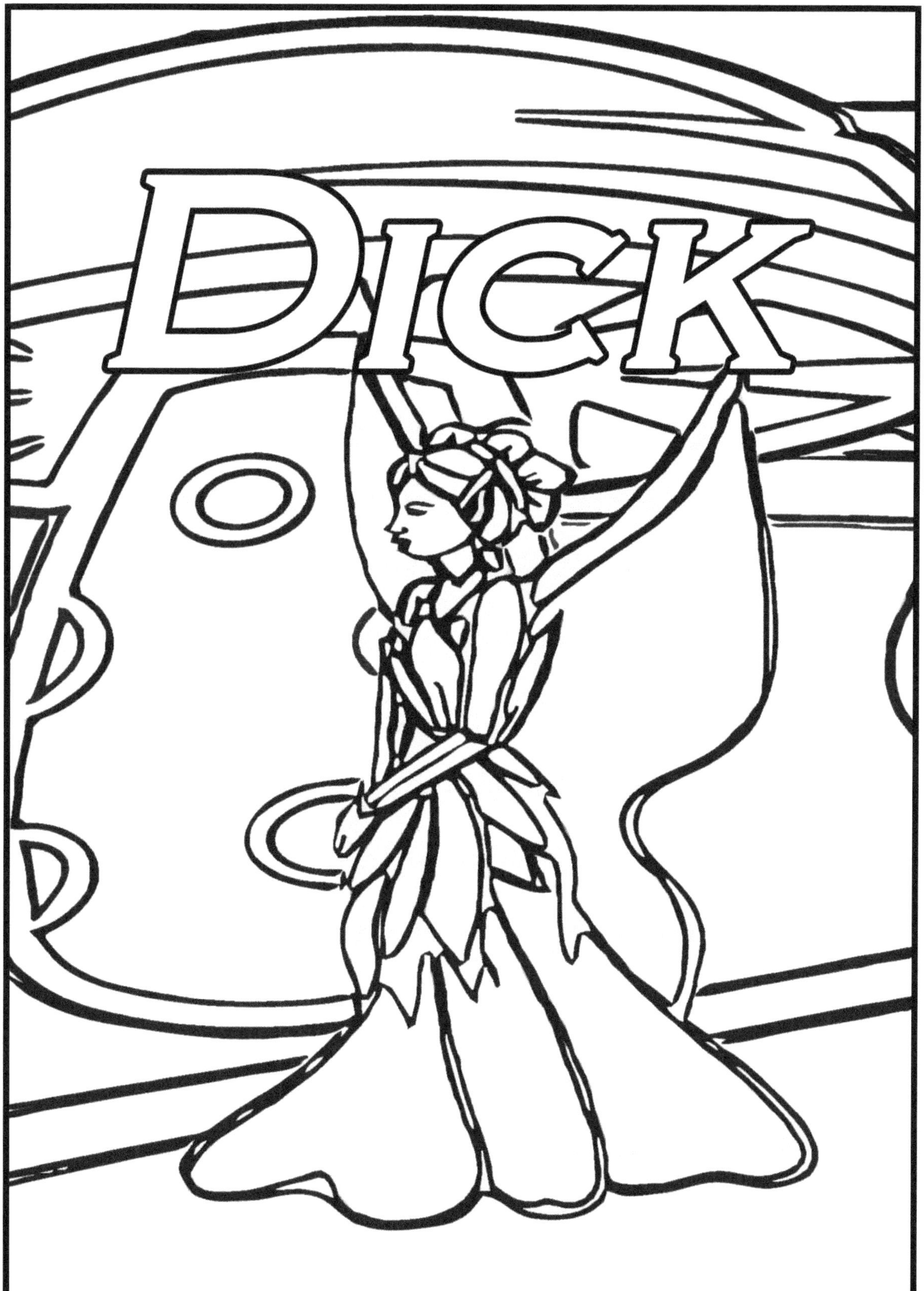
DICK

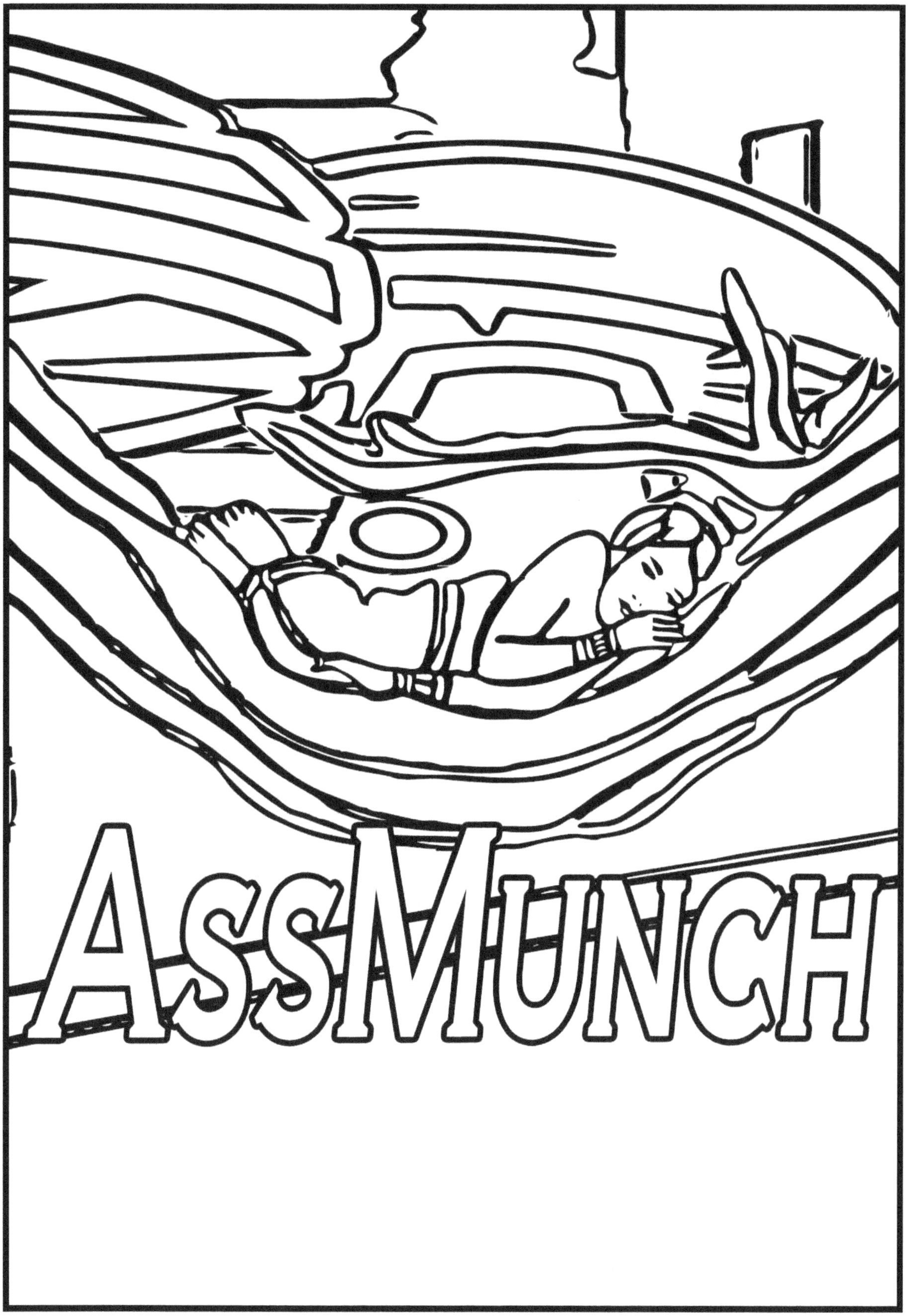
AssMunch

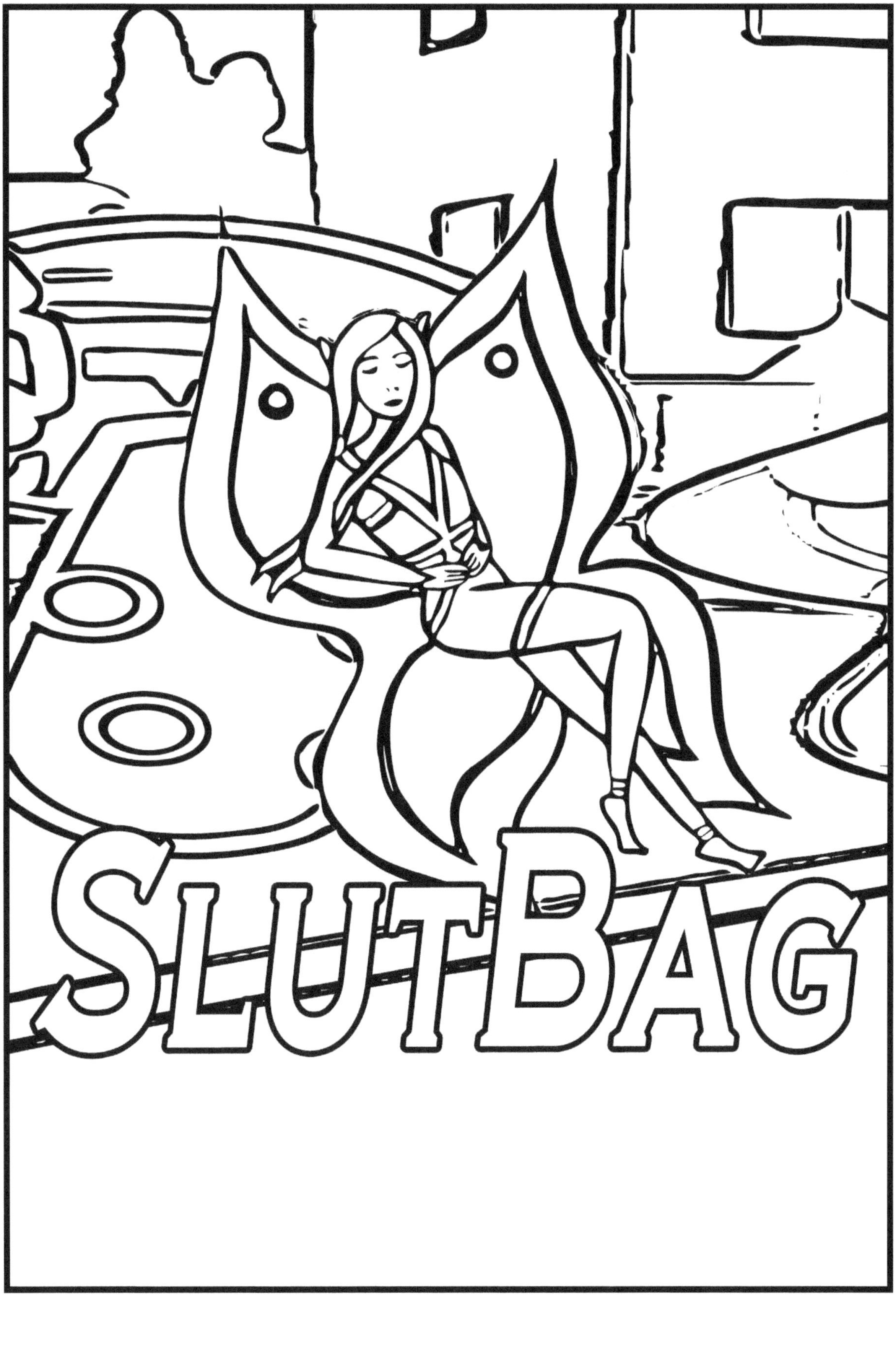
SlutBag

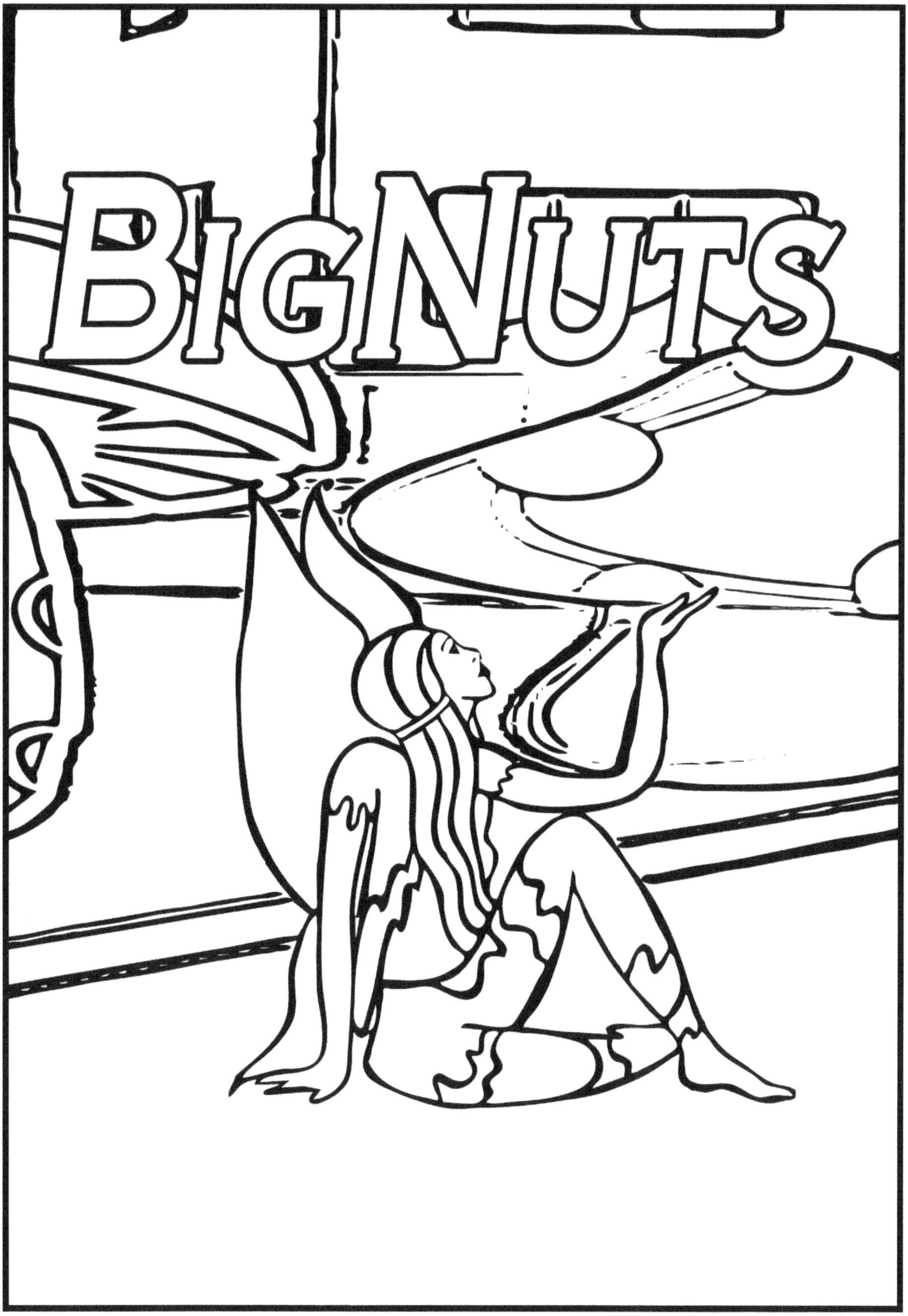
BigNuts

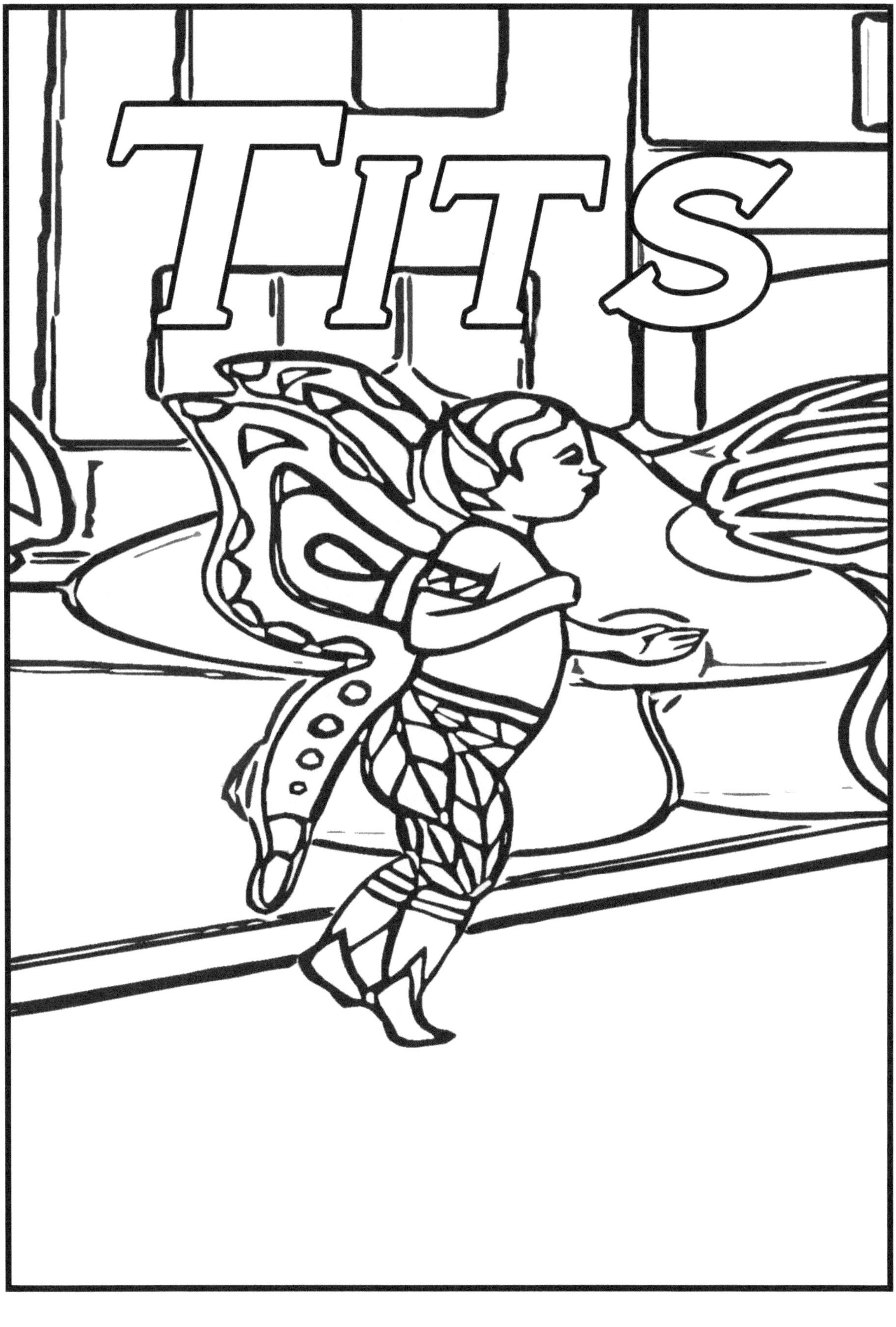
TITS

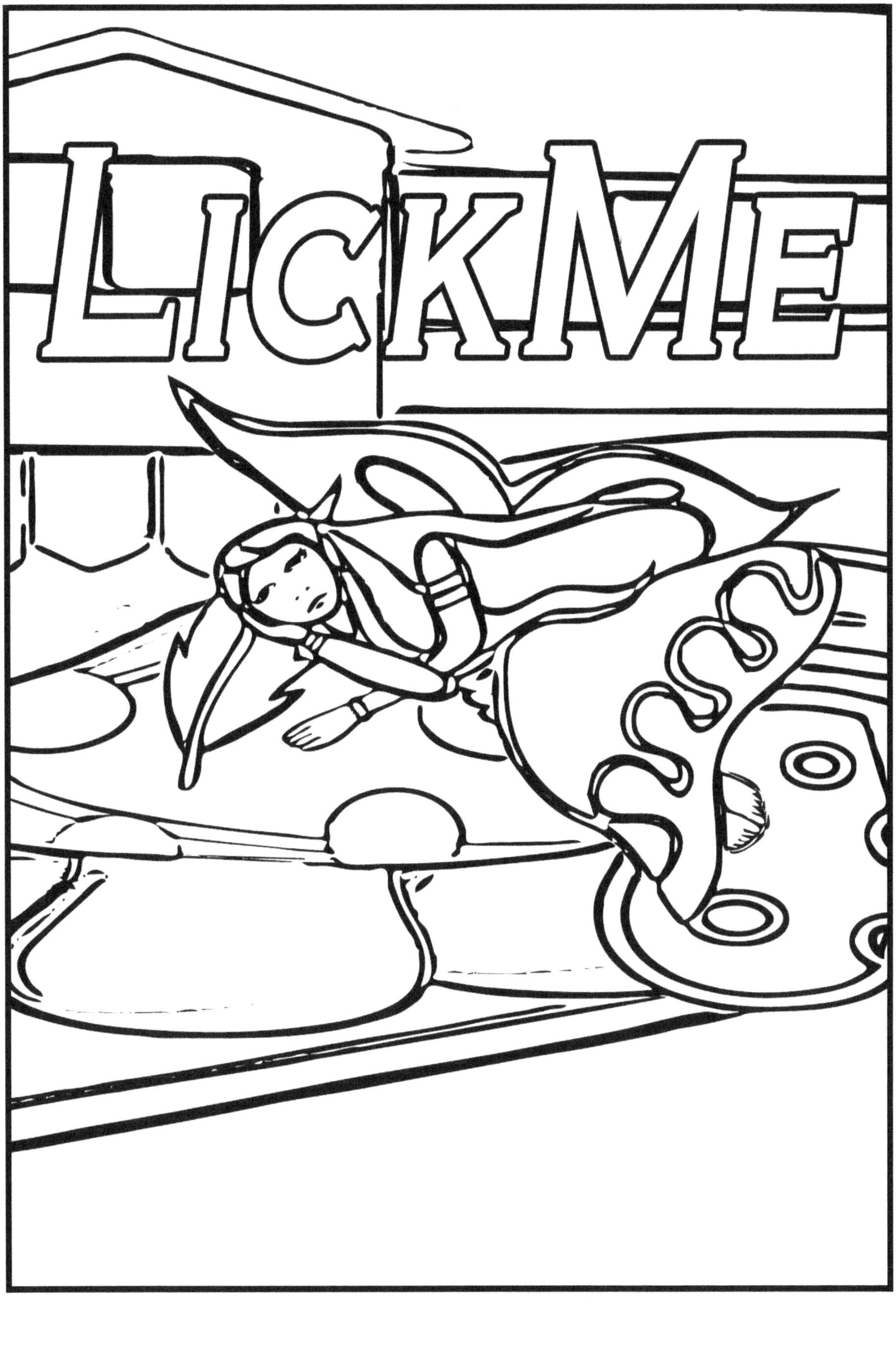
LickMe

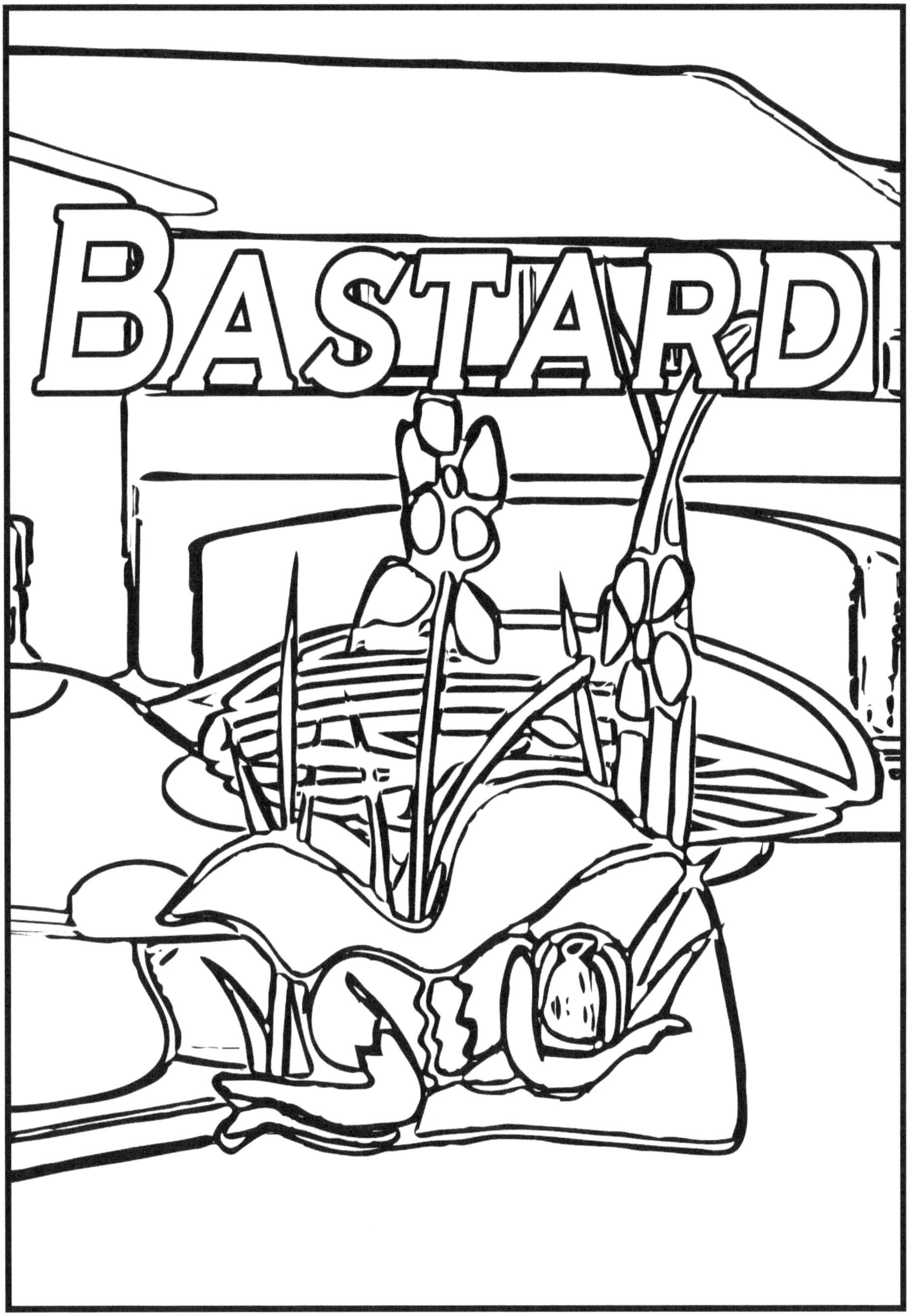
BASTARD

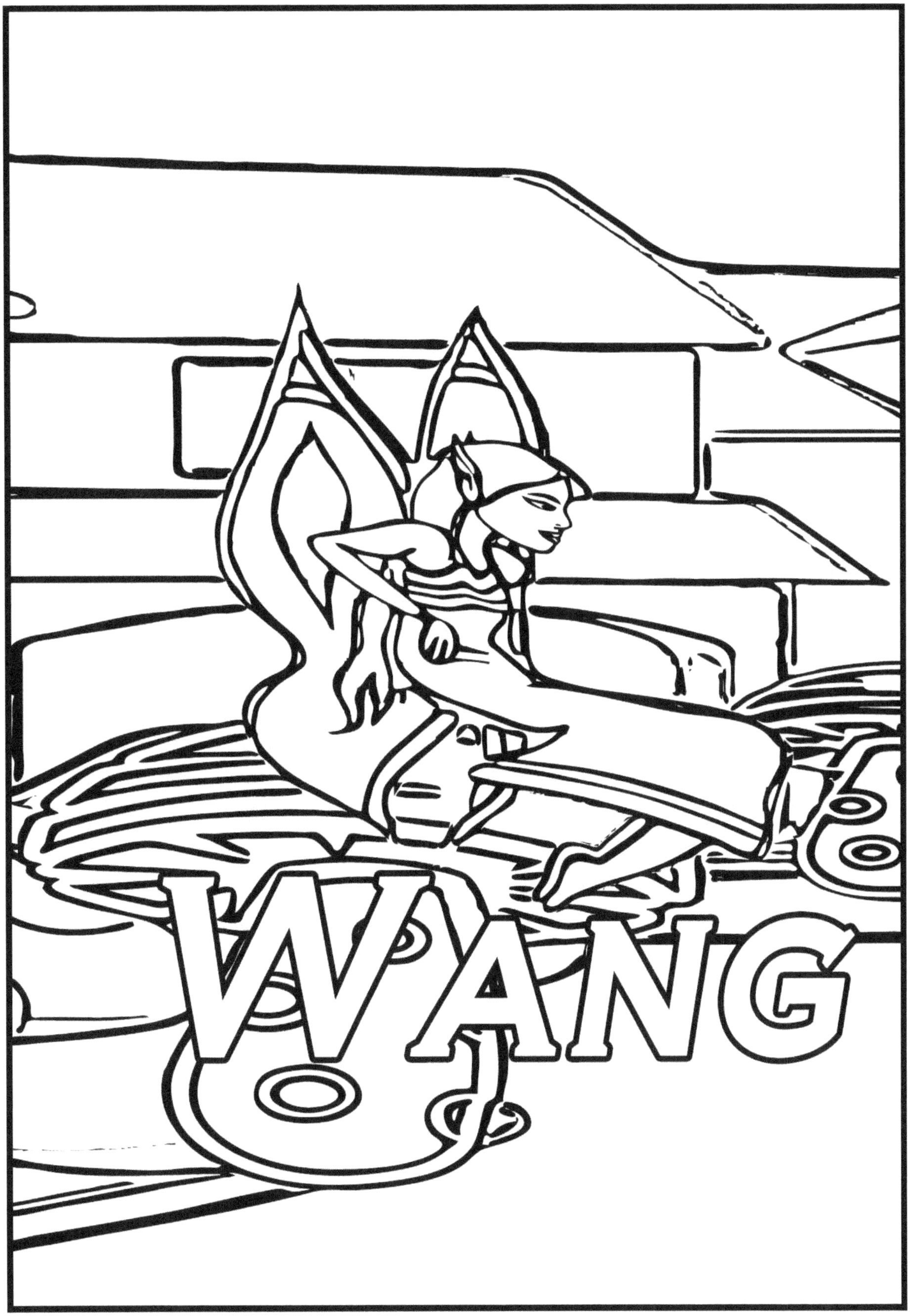
WANG

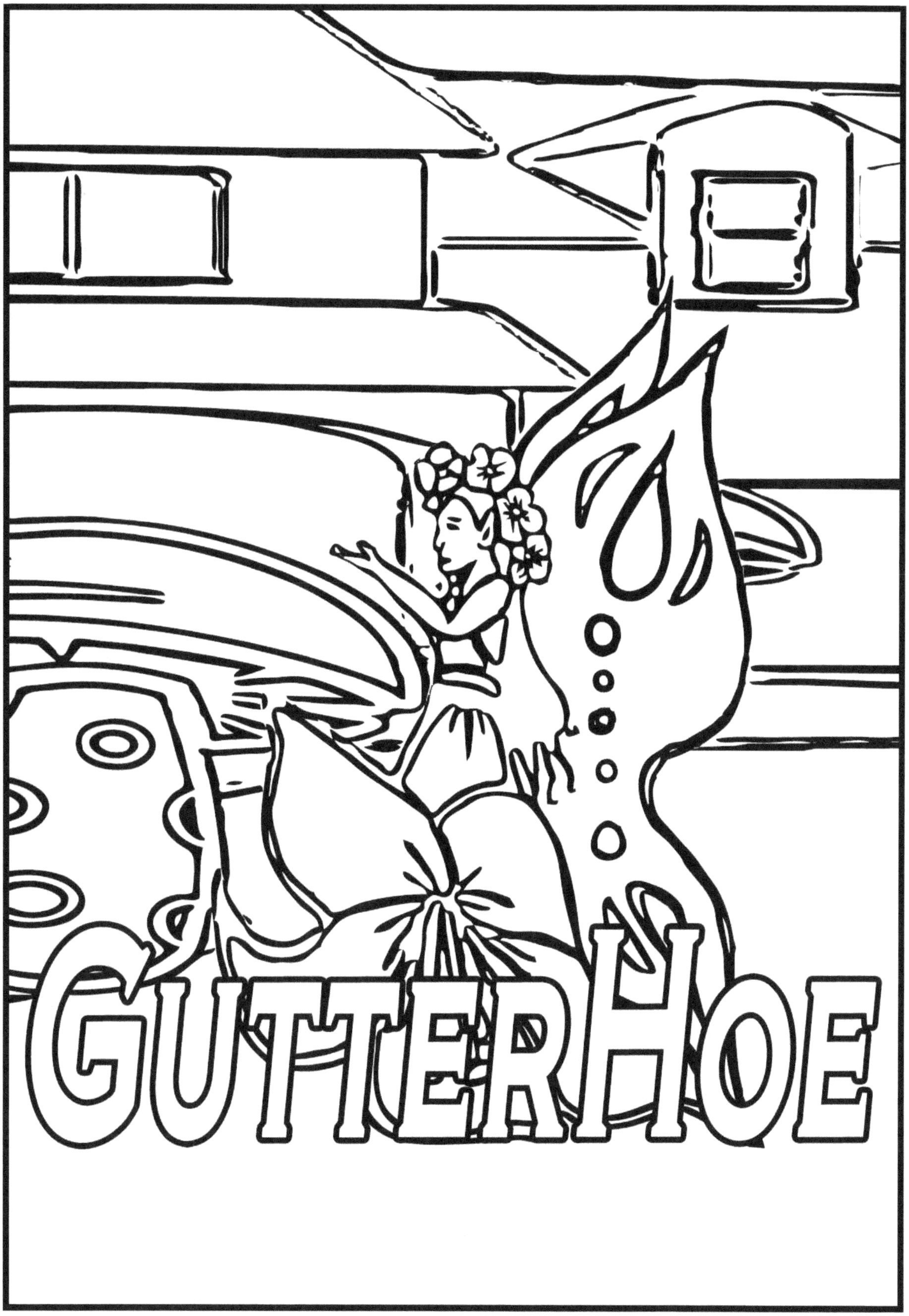
GUTTERHOE

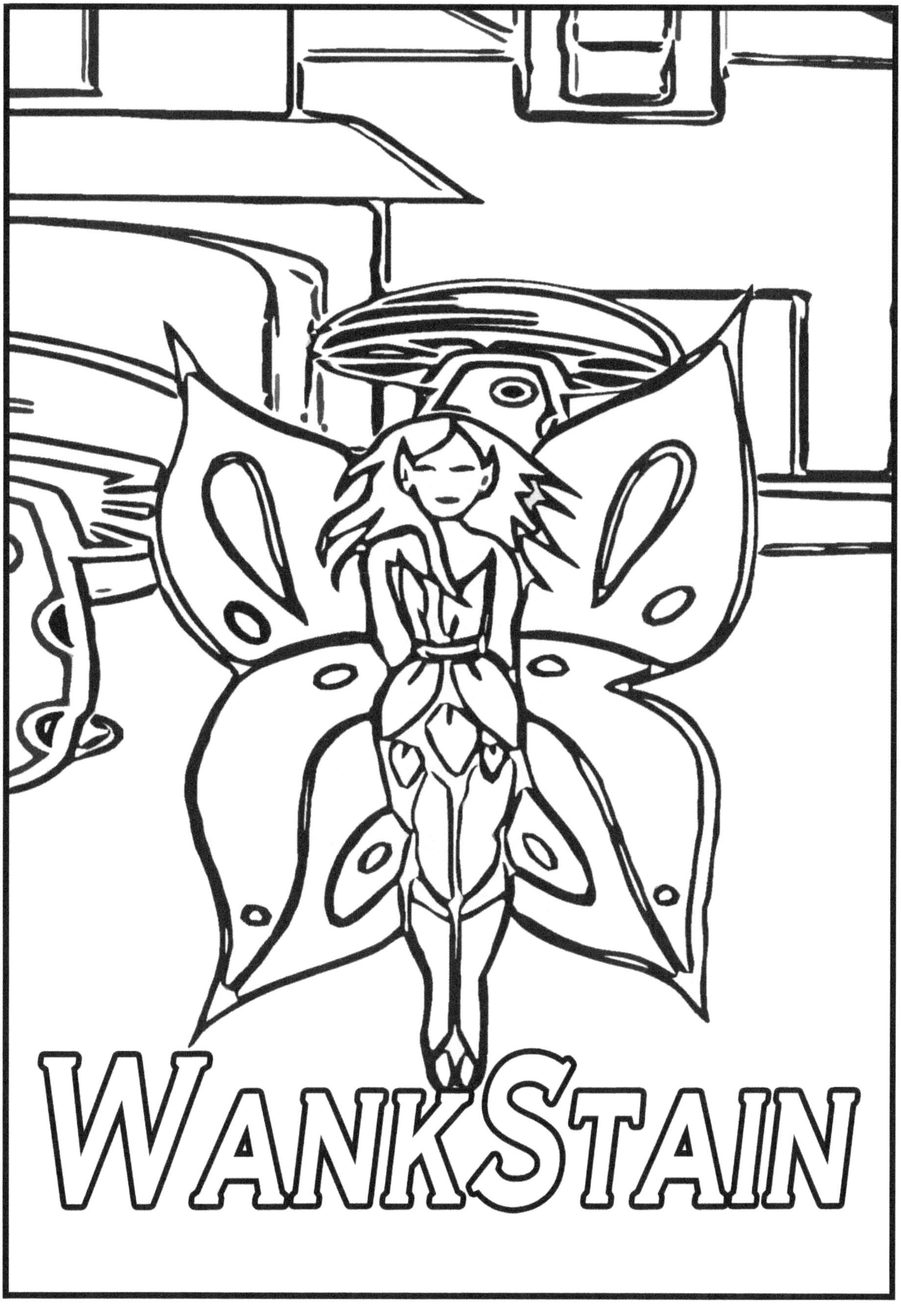
WankStain

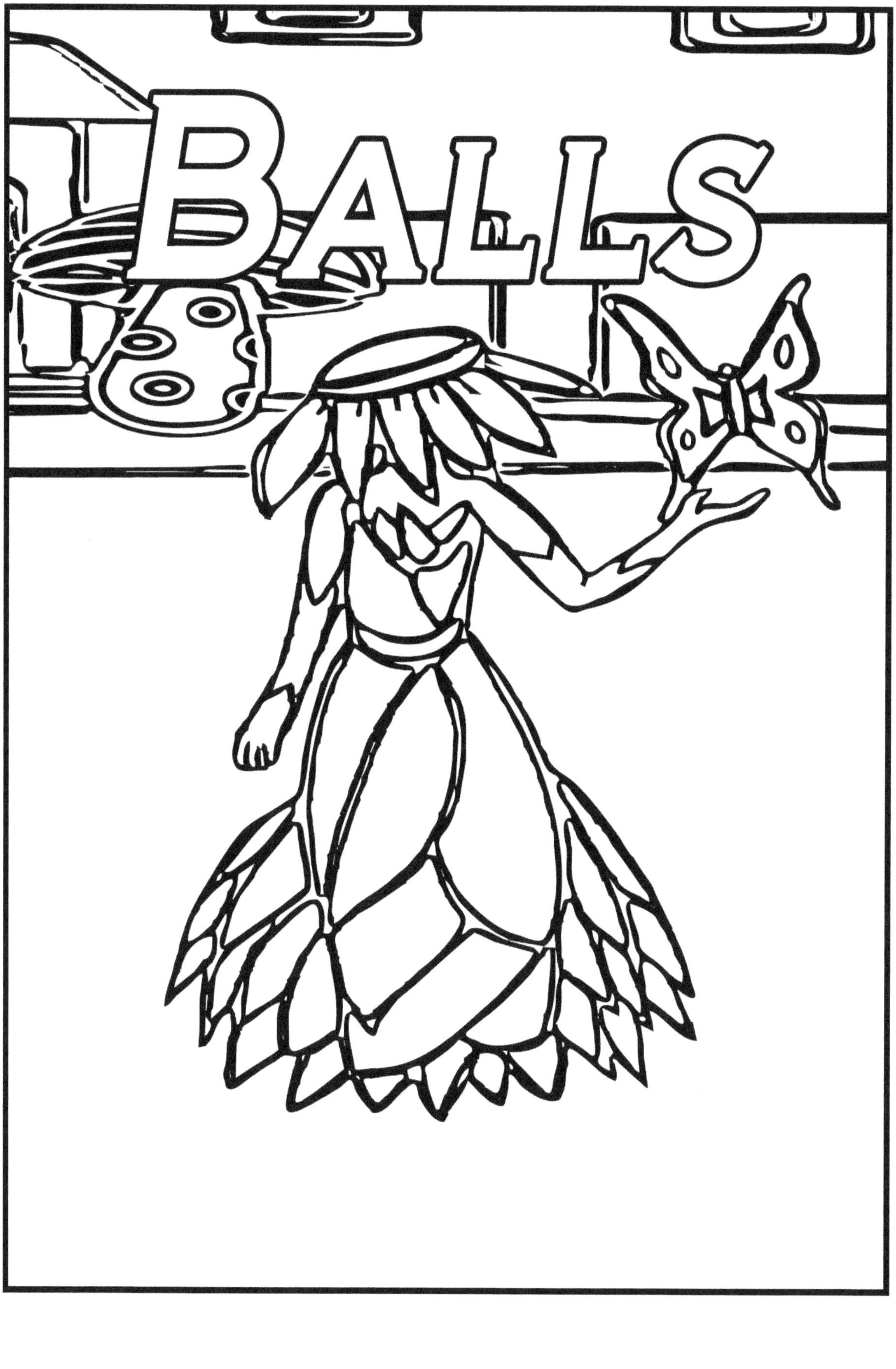
BALLS

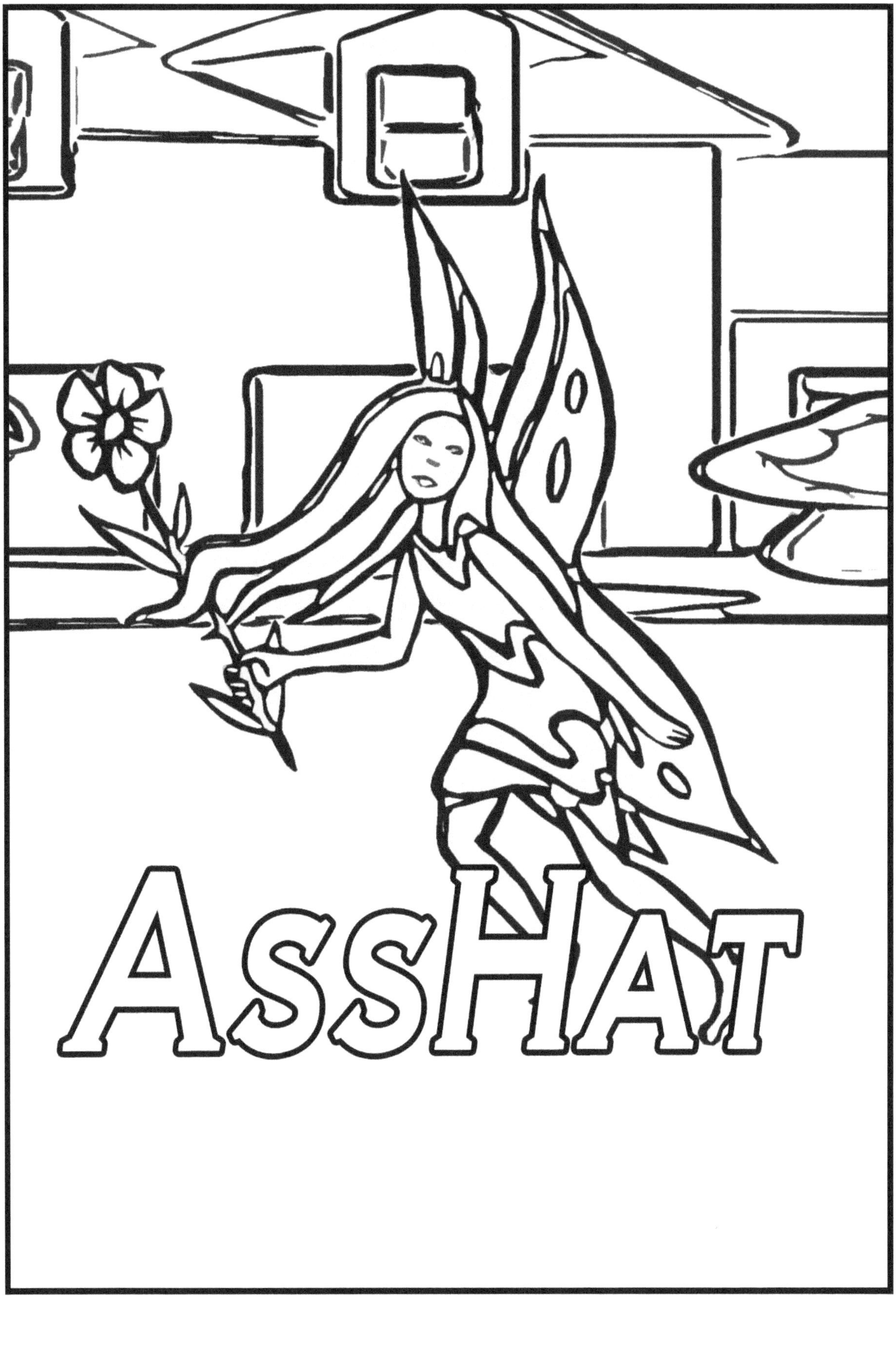
AssHat

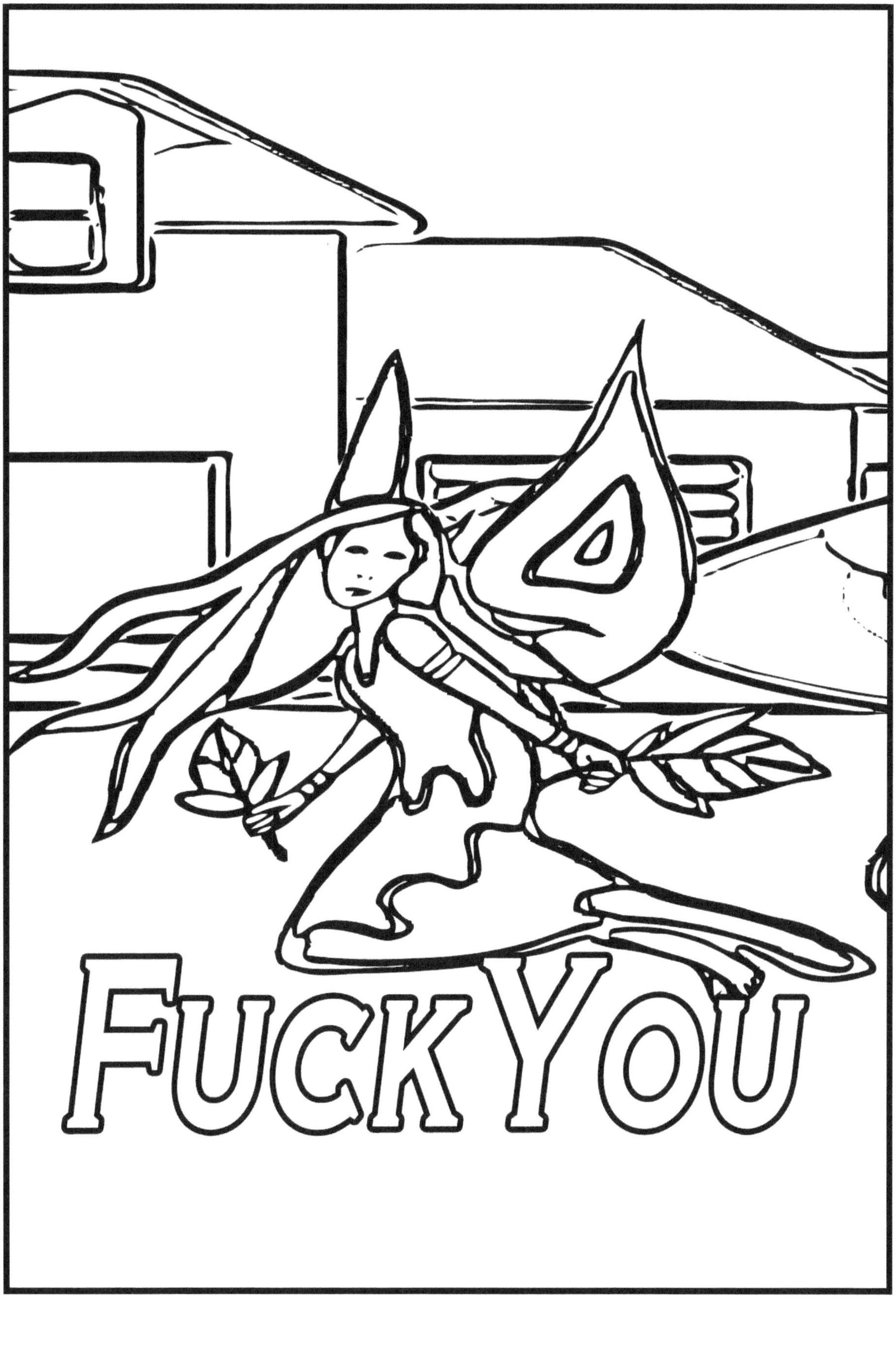
Fuck You

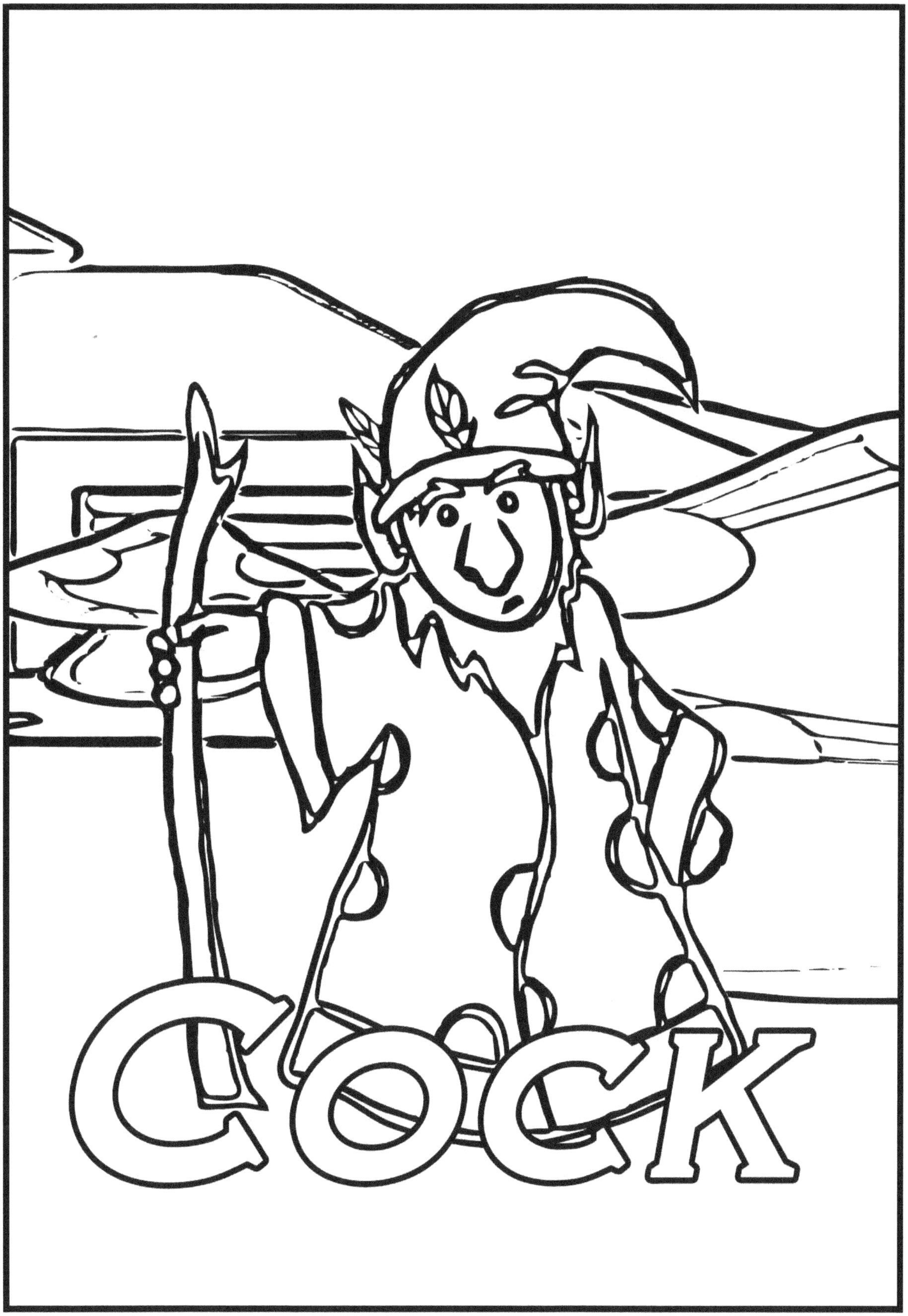
COCK

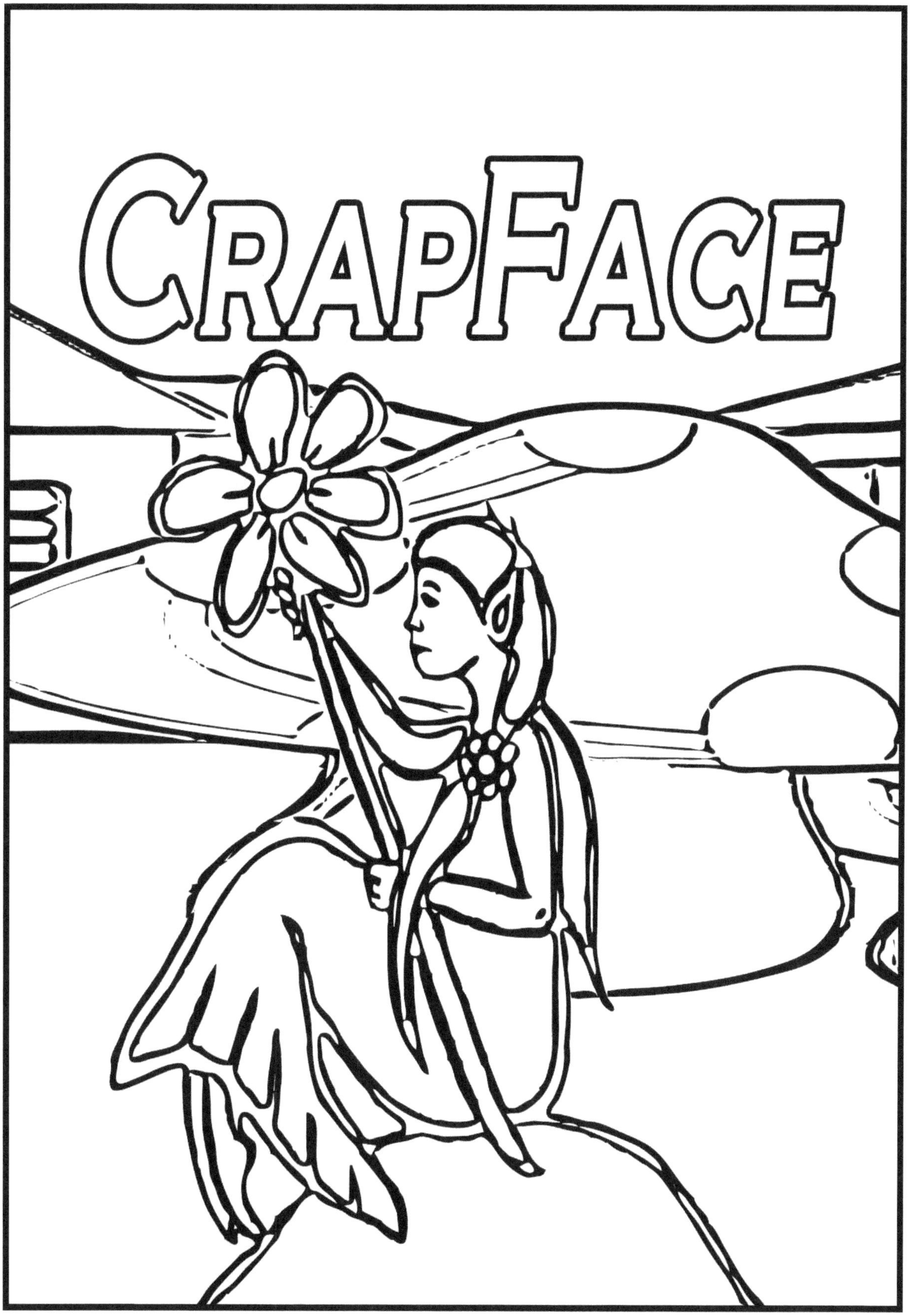
CrapFace

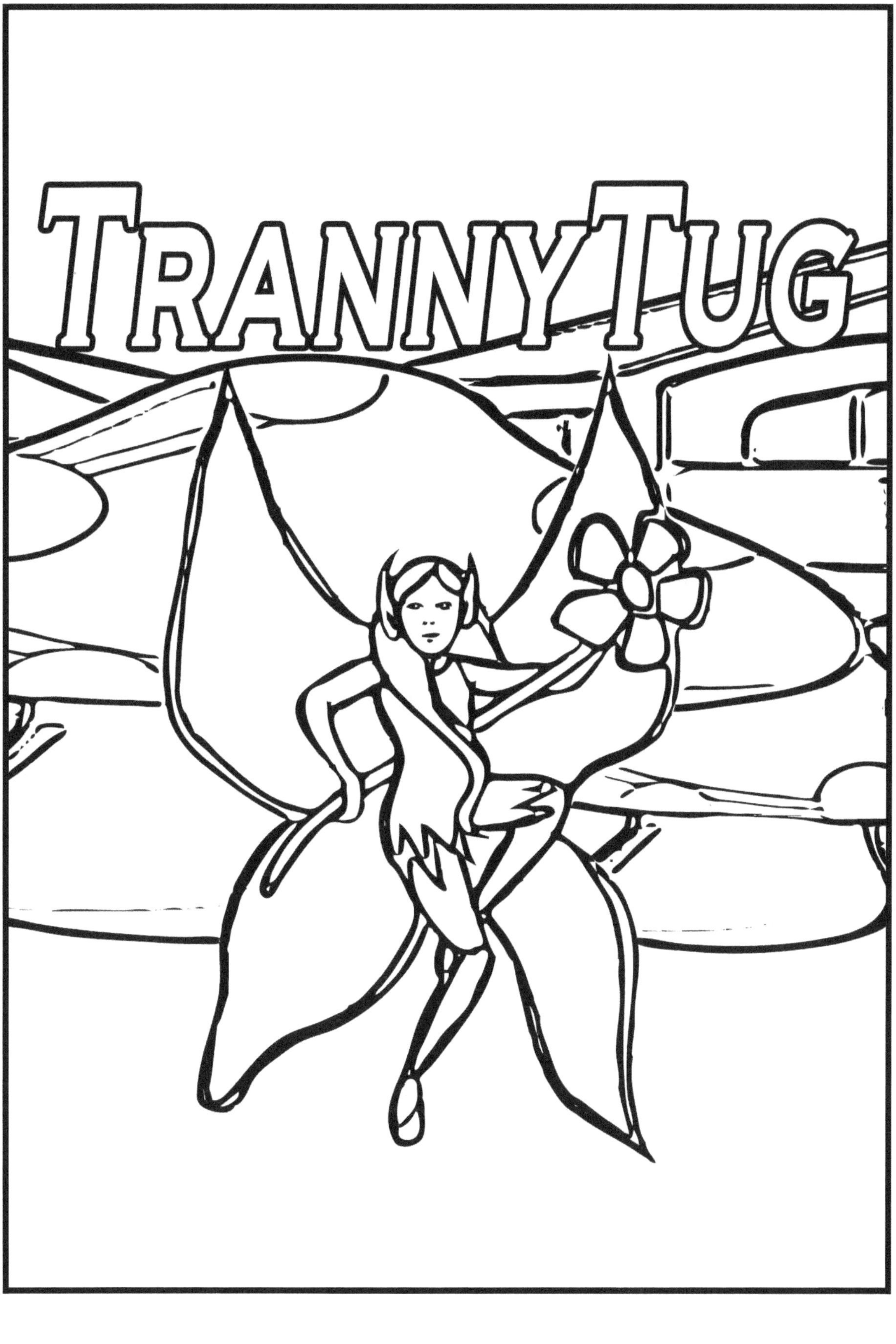
TrannyTug

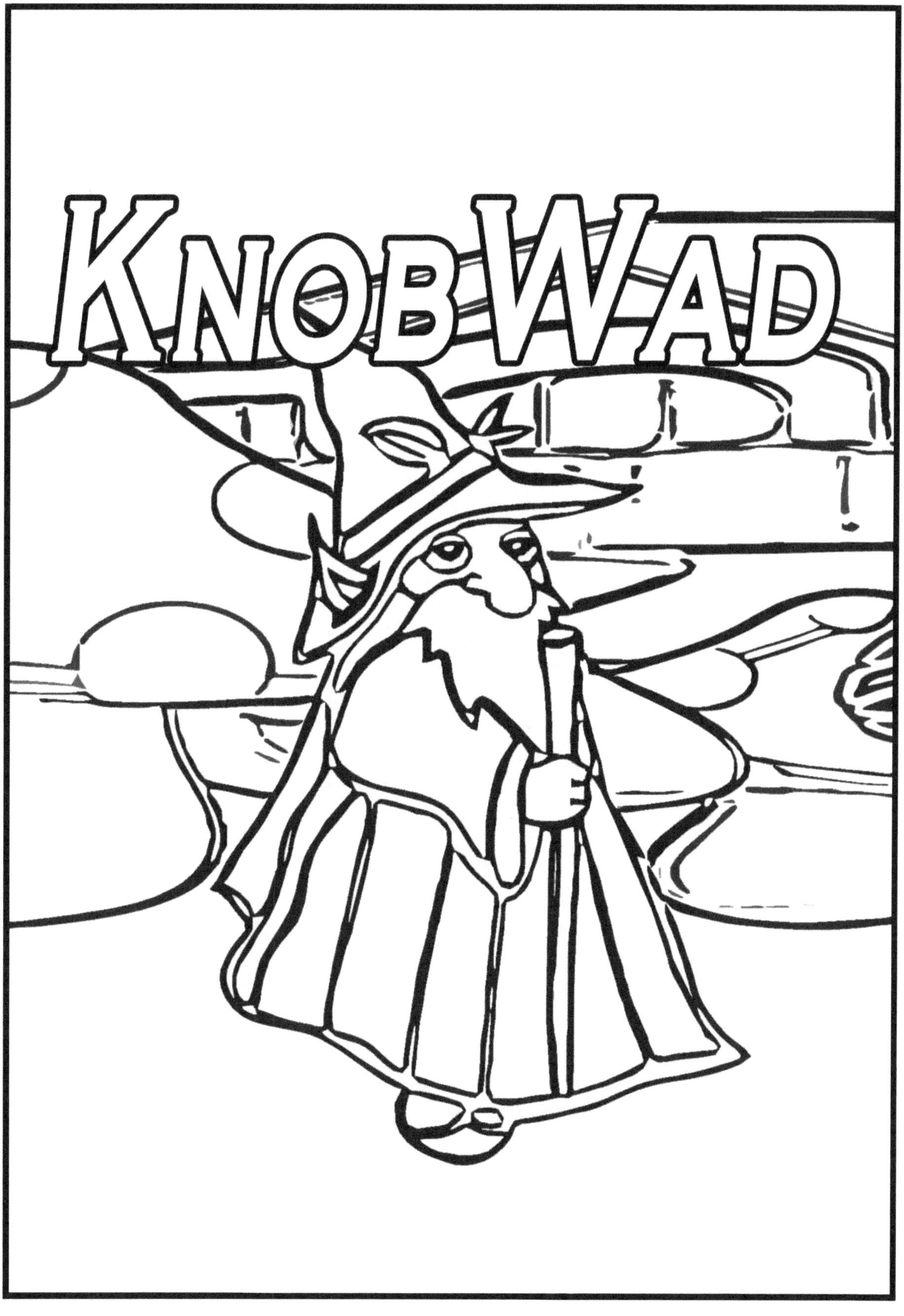
KNOB WAD

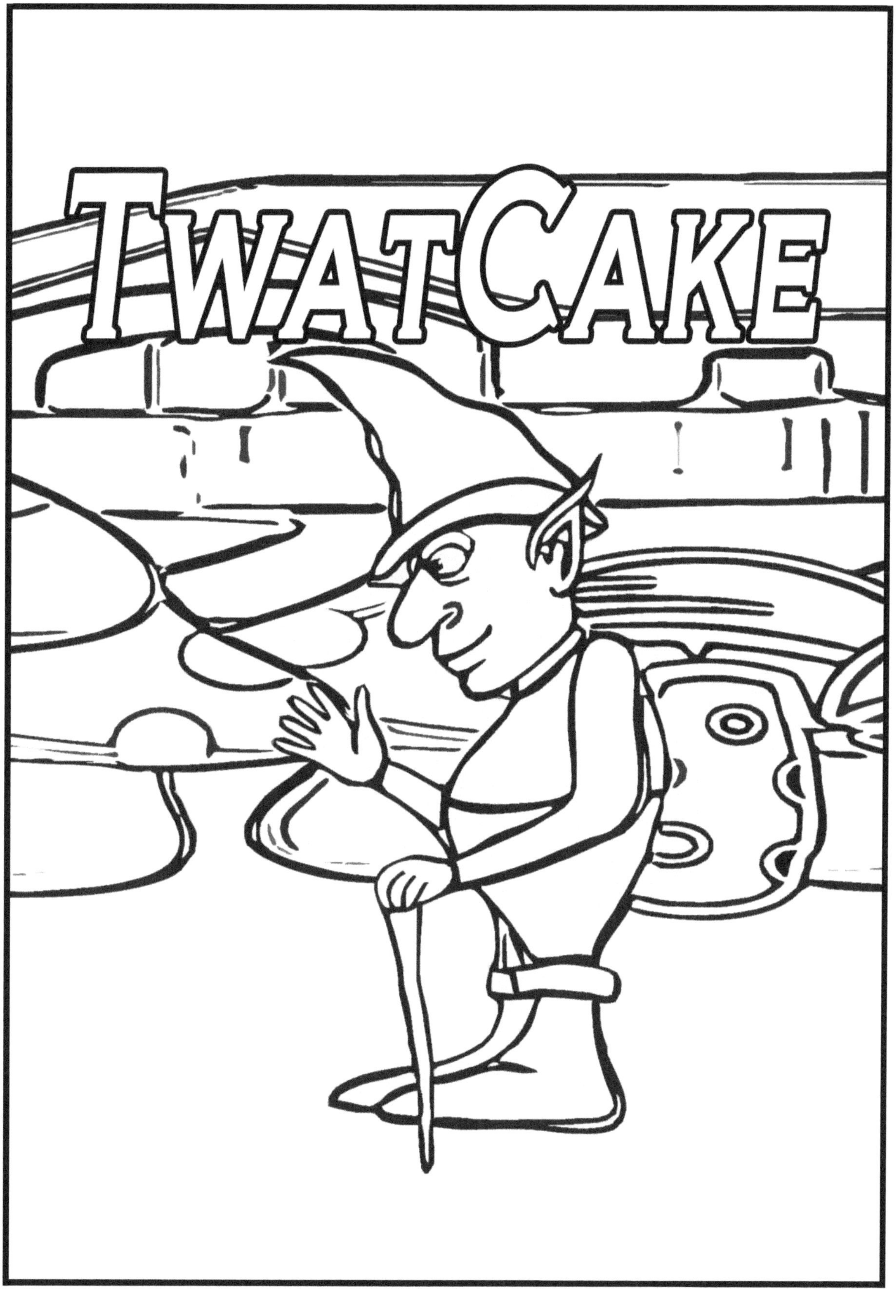
TwatCake

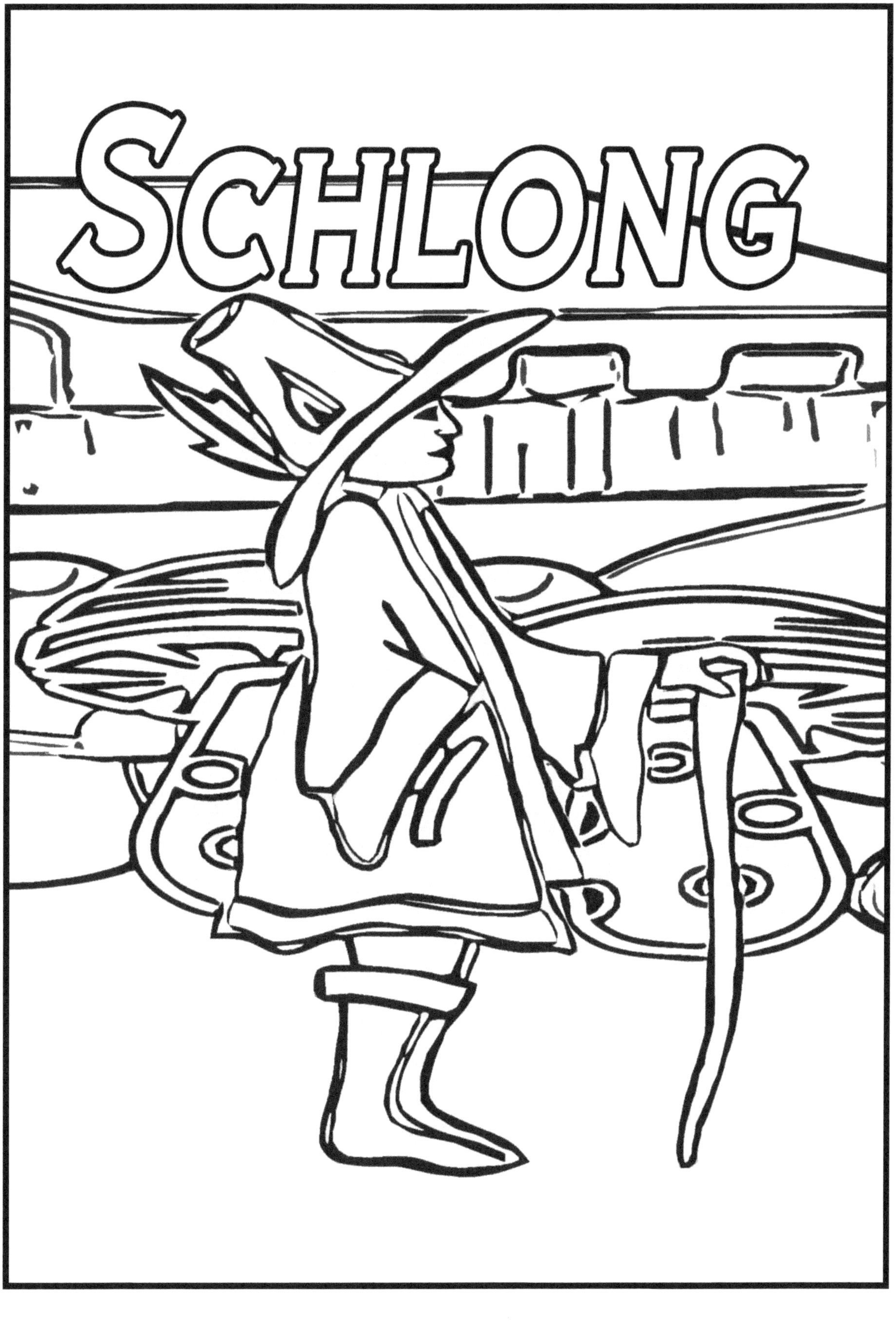
SCHLONG

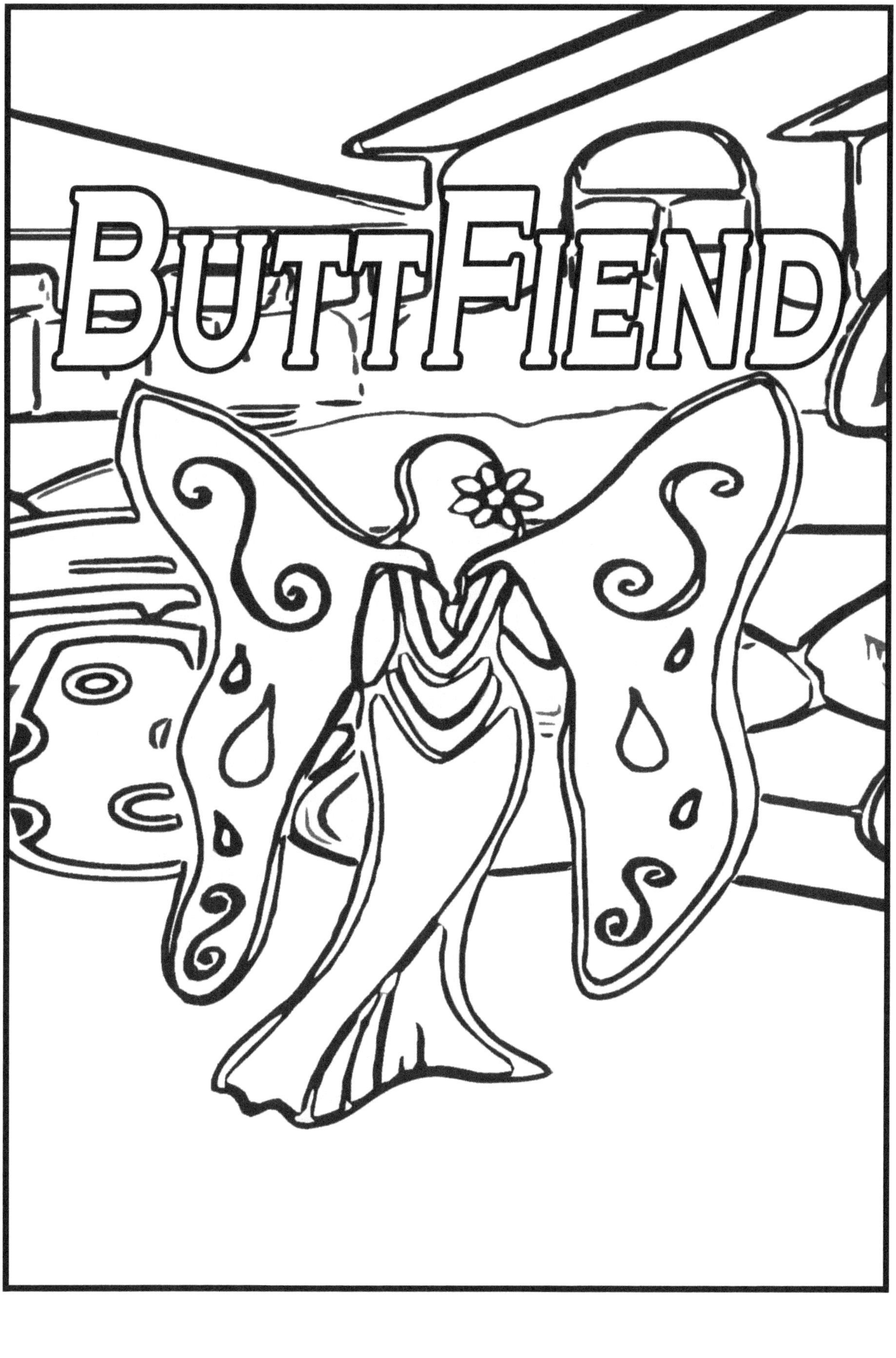
ButtFiend

www.ingramcontent.com/pod-product-compliance
Lightning Source LLC
Chambersburg PA
CBHW080612190526
45169CB00007B/2986